TABLE OF CONT

RUM 2022

A SELECTION OF DELICIOUS COCKTAILS AND RECIPES
EASY TO MAKE

PAUL FRANK

AFTER CARNIVAL DRINK

1 oz. white Barbancourt rum

½ oz. gin

½ oz. sambuca

1 oz. orange juice

½ oz. lemon-lime soda

½ oz. simple syrup

1 kiwi slice

Shake with ice and strain into a highball glass filled with ice cubes.

AFTERBURNER

2 oz. Wray & Nephew rum

½ oz. peppermint schnapps

½ oz. Kahlúa

Pour ingredients into a snifter glass. Swirl to mix.

ALI-COLADA

dash Bacardi rum

2 oz. Alizé liqueur

2 oz. Coco Lopez real cream of coconut

pineapple wedge for garnish

Blend. Garnish with pineapple wedge.

ALNWICK'S 43

½ oz. Alnwick rum

dash orange juice

dash crème de cassis

Shake and pour into a shot glass.

ALOHA

1 oz. dark rum

½ oz. fresh lime juice

2 oz. pineapple juice

2 oz. fresh orange juice

1 oz. Coco Lopez real cream of coconut

small scoop vanilla ice cream

pineapple spear for garnish

maraschino cherry for garnish

Blend. Garnish with pineapple spear and maraschino cherry.

ALPINE GLOW

1 oz. Gosling's Black Seal rum (plus ½ oz. to float)

½ oz. brandy ½ oz. triple sec

2 oz. sweet and sour mix

splash grenadine

lemo twist for garnish

Shake first four ingredients over ice and serve on the rocks. Float ½ oz. Gosling's Black Seal rum and garnish with lemon twist.

ANGOSTURA FUH SO

1 oz. Angostura white rum

1 oz. amaretto

1 oz. heavy cream

fresh cinnamon to taste

3–4 dashes Angostura aromatic bitters

½ oz. grenadine

Blend first five ingredients and layer on grenadine.

ANGOSTURA ROYALE

2 oz. Angostura 1919 premium rum

1 oz. Cointreau

½ oz. blue curaçao

2 oz. pineapple juice

3–4 dashes Angostura aromatic bitters

lime wedges for garnish

Shake and garnish with lime wedges.

ANGOSTURA STINGER

1 oz. Angostura 1919 premium rum

½ oz. white crème de cacao

¼ oz. white crème de menthe

1 oz. heavy cream

dash blue food coloring

3–4 dashes Angostura aromatic bitters

cherries for garnish

parsley for garnish

Shake and garnish with cherries and parsley snips.

APPLE DAIQUIRI

1 oz. light rum

1 oz. apple schnapps

½ oz. sweet and sour mix

¼ apple, peeled

apple slice for garnish

Blend. Garnish with apple slice.

APPLE PIE À LA MODE

¾ oz. Captain Morgan original spiced rum

½ oz. apple schnapps

2 oz. apple juice

2 tbsp. apple pie filling

1 oz. cream of coconut

1 oz. heavy cream

16-oz. scoop crushed ice

cinnamon for sprinkling

apple wedge or cinnamon stick for garnish

Blend until smooth and creamy. Serve in specialty glass. Garnish with apple wedge or cinnamon stick.

APPLESAUCE

1 oz. Captain Morgan original spiced rum

3 oz. applesauce

4 oz. sweet and sour mix/margarita mix

¼ oz. triple sec

Blend with 12 oz. ice until slushy. Serve in a 15-oz. glass.

APPLETON BLUE LAGOON

1½ oz. Appleton Estate V/X Jamaica rum

1 oz. blue curaçao

5 oz. lemonade

lime wedge for garnish

Pour into a highball or Collins glass over ice and stir. Garnish with lime wedge.

APPLETON BOSSA NOVA

1½ oz. Appleton Estate V/X rum

¼ oz. lime juice

¼ oz. lemon juice

5 oz. passion fruit juice

orange slice for garnish

Combine in a shaker and mix well. Serve in a colada glass over ice. Garnish with orange slice.

APPLETON CARIBBEAN COSMO

1½ oz. Appleton Estate V/X Jamaica rum

¾ oz. triple sec

splash lime juice

cranberry juice to taste

Mix well and pour into a rocks glass over ice.

APPLETON CARIBBEAN SEA

1½ oz. Appleton Estate V/X Jamaica rum

¾ oz. blue curacao

3 oz. pineapple juice

1½ oz. coconut cream

pineapple wedge for garnish

cherry for garnish

Blend with ice. Serve in a cocktail or margarita glass and garnish with pineapple wedge and cherry.

APPLETON COSMO ENCOUNTER

1½ oz. Appleton Estate V/X Jamaica rum

½ oz. triple sec

splash lime juice

cranberry juice to taste

lime twist for garnish

Mix well and serve in a martini glass. Garnish with a twist of lime.

APPLETON DOCTOR BIRD

1½ oz. Appleton Estate V/X Jamaica rum

3 oz. pineapple juice

1 tsp. sugar

½ lime

3 oz. ginger ale

pineapple wedge for garnish

cherry for garnish

Cut up the lime. Blend with first three ingredients and mix until smooth. Pour into a Collins or rocks glass, top with ginger ale, and garnish with pineapple wedge and cherry.

APPLETON ELUSIVE REDHEAD

1½ oz. Appleton Estate V/X Jamaica rum

3 oz. Clamato or Bloody Mary mix

horseradish to taste

Tabasco to taste

sea salt to taste, plus more to rim glass

black pepper to taste, plus more to rim glass

Worcestershire sauce to taste

lime juice to taste

celery stick for garnish

olives for garnish

Tomolives for garnish

Season to taste with horseradish, Tabasco, pepper, sea salt, Worcestershire sauce, and lime juice. Rim glass in sea salt and/or pepper. Pour into glass. Garnish with a celery stick, olives, and Tomolives.

APPLETON ESTATE V/X AND SODA/TONIC

2 oz. Appleton Estate V/X Jamaica rum

½ oz. sherry

drizzle of sweet vermouth

maraschino cherry for garnish

Pour rum into a rocks glass over ice, add sherry and sweet vermouth, and garnish with maraschino cherry.

APPLETON ESTATE V/X
CLASSIC BANANA DAIQUIRI

2 oz. Appleton Estate V/X Jamaica rum

½ oz. fresh lime juice

1 oz. banana liqueur

¼ oz. simple syrup lime slice for garnish

Shake with ice and strain into a martini glass. Garnish with a lime slice.

APPLETON ESTATE V/X
CLASSIC MAI TAI

1 oz. Appleton Estate V/X Jamaica rum

1 oz. Appleton Estate Reserve Jamaica rum

½ oz. apricot brandy

½ oz. orange curaçao

dash grenadine

dash orgeat syrup

3 oz. fresh pineapple juice

½ oz. dark Coruba Jamaica rum (optional)

mint sprig for garnish

Shake with ice until foamy and pour into a Collins glass. Float dark Coruba Jamaica rum on top and garnish with a mint sprig.

APPLETON ESTATE V/X COSMOPOLITAN

1½ oz. Appleton Estate V/X Jamaica rum

½ oz. triple sec

splash lime juice

cranberry juice to taste

lime twist for garnish

Shake with ice and strain into a martini glass. Garnish with a twist of lime.

APPLETON ESTATE V/X HURRICANE

1½ oz. Appleton Estate V/X Jamaica rum

1½ oz. Coruba dark rum

splash Rose's lime juice

¼ oz. simple syrup

2 oz. fresh orange juice

2 oz. fresh pineapple juice

orange wheel for garnish

lime zest for garnish

lemon zest for garnish

Mix well and strain into a hurricane glass. Garnish with an orange wheel, lime zest, and lemon zest.

APPLETON ESTATE V/X MANHATTAN

2 oz. Appleton Estate V/X Jamaica rum

4 oz. soda

lime or lemon wedge for garnish

Pour into a rocks glass over ice. Garnish with a fresh lime or lemon wedge.

APPLETON ESTATE V/X PLANTER'S PUNCH

1½ oz. Appleton Estate V/X Jamaica rum

½ oz. grenadine

2 dashes Angostura bitters

1½ oz. sweet and sour mix

1½ oz. orange juice

orange wedge for garnish

cherry for garnish

Build in a tall glass over ice and stir. Garnish with orange wedge and cherry.

APPLETON EXOTIC LADY

1½ oz. Appleton Estate V/X Jamaica rum

2 oz. pineapple juice

2 oz. ginger ale

¼ oz. grenadine

½ lime

1 tsp. sugar

pineapple wedge for garnish

cherry for garnish

Cut up lime and mix with pineapple juice, rum, sugar, and grenadine over ice. Strain into a martini glass and top with ginger ale. Garnish with pineapple wedge and cherry.

APPLETON EXQUISITE DAIQUIRI

2 oz. Appleton Estate V/X Jamaica rum

½ oz. fresh lime juice

¼ oz. simple syrup

lime slice for garnish

Shake with ice and strain into a martini glass. Garnish with lime slice.

APPLETON GREEN PARROT

1½ oz. Appleton Estate V/X Jamaica rum

4 oz. orange juice

1 oz. blue curacao

orange slice for garnish

Pour ingredients one at a time in the order listed above into a stemware glass over ice. Do not mix. Garnish with orange slice.

APPLETON ISLAND ENTICEMENT

1 oz. Appleton Estate V/X Jamaica rum

1 oz. Midori melon liqueur

3 oz. pineapple juice

splash grenadine

pineapple wedge for garnish

cherry for garnish

Stir first three ingredients with ice. Pour into a glass, then float grenadine on top. Garnish with pineapple wedge and cherry.

APPLETON JAMAICA SUNSET

1½ oz. Appleton Estate V/X Jamaica rum

2½ oz. cranberry juice

3½ oz. orange juice

orange wheel for garnish

Pour first two ingredients into a highball or stemware glass over ice. Slowly add orange juice. Garnish with orange wheel.

APPLETON JAMAICAN ECSTASY DREAM

½ oz. Appleton Estate V/X Jamaica rum

½ oz. cranberry juice

½ oz. grapefruit juice

½ oz. orange juice

½ oz. club soda

orange wedge for garnish

In a highball glass, pour rum, cranberry juice, and grapefruit juice over ice. Slowly add orange juice and top with club soda. Garnish with orange wedge.

APPLETON JAMAICAN MARTINI

3 oz. Appleton Estate V/X Jamaica rum

1½ oz. lime juice

½ tsp. grenadine or strawberry syrup

lime wedge for garnish

Spoon grenadine into a chilled cocktail glass. Stir rum and lime over ice in a separate mixing glass and strain into the cocktail glass. Garnish with lime wedge.

APPLETON PURPLE DEW

1½ oz. Appleton Estate V/X Jamaica rum

3 oz. cranberry juice

1 oz. clear syrup

1 oz. blue curaçao

1 oz. lime juice

pineapple wedge for garnish

cherry for garnish

Stir in a Collins or punch glass over ice. Garnish with pineapple wedge and cherry.

APPLETON YELLOW BIRD

1½ oz. Appleton Estate V/X Jamaica rum

3 oz. pineapple juice

½ oz. orange juice

¾ oz. crème de banana

½ oz. apricot brandy

orange slice for garnish

Mix well. Strain into a Collins glass over ice and garnish with orange slice.

APRICOT PIÑA

1½ oz. light rum

½ oz. apricot brandy

1½ oz. unsweetened pineapple juice

1 oz. Coco Lopez real cream of coconut

Blend.

ARCHANGEL

2 oz. Wray & Nephew rum

¼ oz. strawberry puree

½ oz. peach schnapps

½ oz. cachaca

½ oz. pineapple juice

4 basil leaves for garnish

Shake with ice and strain into a Collins glass over ice. Garnish with basil leaves.

ARIANA'S DREAM

½ oz. Bacardi rum

1 oz. Alizé liqueur

1 oz. crème de cacao

3 oz. orange juice

fresh strawberry for garnish

Garnish with fresh strawberry.

ASSAM CHAI PUNCH

1½ oz. Pyrat XO Reserve rum

½ oz. Grand Marnier

1 oz. orange juice

1 oz. fresh sweet and sour

3 oz. chai tea

orange twist for garnish

mint sprig for garnish

Shake and strain over ice. Garnish with orange twist and fresh mint sprig.

BACARDI AMBER DAIQUIRI

2 oz. Bacardi dark rum

2 tsp. fresh lime or lemon juice

½ tsp. sugar

½ tsp. cream

grated nutmeg for garnish

Blend and serve in a tall glass. Garnish with nutmeg.

BACARDI ANCIENT MARINER

Equal parts:

Bacardi Gold Reserve rum

Grand Marnier

Stir with ice. Serve straight up or in a martini glass.

BACARDI BANANA COLADA

1½ oz. Bacardi light or dark rum

1 oz. Coco Lopez real cream of coconut

½ ripe banana

Blend with ½ cup ice or shake and serve on ice.

BACARDI BIG APPLE

1½ oz. Bacardi light or dark rum

¾ oz. lemon or lime juice

½ oz. apple brandy

¾ oz. grenadine

apple slice for garnish

Shake with ice and serve in a tall glass with ice. Garnish with apple slice.

BACARDI BLACK DIRTY COLADA

1¼ oz. Bacardi black rum

1 oz. Coco Lopez real cream of coconut

2 oz. pineapple juice

Blend.

BACARDI BLACK RUSSIAN

1 part coffee liqueur

2 parts Bacardi light rum

Stir over ice in a rocks glass.

BACARDI BLOSSOM

1¼oz. Bacardi light rum

1 oz. orange juice

½ oz. lemon juice

½ tsp. sugar

BACARDI CHAMPAGNE COCKTAIL

1 oz. Bacardi silver rum

1 tsp. sugar

dash bitters

champagne to fill

Mix first three ingredients in a tall glass. Fill with champagne.

BACARDI COCKTAIL

3 parts Bacardi Superior rum

1 part lemon juice

1 tsp. grenadine

1 tbsp. sugar

Mix until ice has a consistency of sherbet. Serve in a stemmed cocktail glass.

BACARDI COLLINS

2 oz. Bacardi light rum

2 tsp. frozen lemonade or limeade (or juice of ½ lime or lemon)

½ tsp. sugar (1 tsp. if fresh lime or lemon juice is used)

club soda to fill

sliced fruit for garnish

cherry for garnish

Pour juices into a shaker over ice. Add sugar and Bacardi light rum. Shake well and pour into a tall glass. Fill with club soda and stir. Garnish with fruit slices and cherry.

BACARDI DAIQUIRI

1¼ oz. Bacardi light rum

½ oz. lemon juice

½ tsp. sugar

Mix in a shaker or blend with ice. Strain into a chilled cocktail glass or serve on the rocks. The original daiquiri was made with Bacardi rum in 1896.

BACARDI DRIVER

2 oz. Bacardi light rum

orange juice to fill

lime or lemon wedge

Pour Bacardi light rum into a tall glass over ice. Fill with orange juice. Squeeze and drop in a lime or lemon wedge. Stir.

BACARDI DRY MARTINI

2–3 oz. Bacardi dark or Gold Reserve rum

1 part dry vermouth

cherry for garnish

Stir with cracked ice and strain into a cocktail glass or pour over rocks. Garnish with cherry.

BACARDI EGGNOG BOWL

12 oz. Bacardi dark or Bacardi Gold Reserve rum

1 qt. fresh or canned eggnog

1 cup whipped heavy cream

grated nutmeg for garnish

Pour eggnog into a punch bowl. Add Bacardi dark or Bacardi Gold Reserve rum. Stir. Fold in whipping cream. Chill in refrigerator. Stir. Top individual servings with nutmeg and serve immediately. Serves 6.

BACARDI FIRESIDE

1¼ oz. Bacardi light or dark rum

1 tsp. sugar

hot tea to fill

1 cinnamon stick

Pour first two ingredients into a mug. Fill with very hot tea and add cinnamon stick. Stir.

BACARDI FIZZ

1¼ oz. Bacardi light rum

¼ oz. lemon juice

¼ oz. Rose's grenadine

soda to fill

Pour first two ingredients into a highball glass over ice. Add the grenadine and fill with soda.

BACARDI GIMLET

1 part Rose's lime juice

4 parts Bacardi light rum

thin slice lime for garnish

Stir over ice. Serve in cocktail glass with lime slice.

BACARDI HEMINGWAY

1½ oz. Bacardi light rum

juice of ½ lime

¼ oz. grapefruit juice

¼ oz. maraschino liqueur

Mix.

BACARDI HIGHBALL

2 oz. Bacardi light, dark, or Gold Reserve rum

club soda, water, or ginger ale to fill

Pour Bacardi over ice cubes in a highball glass. Fill with club soda, water, or ginger ale.

BACARDI KEY LARGO

1½ oz. Bacardi dark rum

2 oz. orange juice

1½ oz. Coco Lopez real cream of coconut

maraschino cherry for garnish

Garnish with a maraschino cherry.

BACARDI MAI TAI

½ oz. fresh lime juice

½ oz. orgeat syrup

½ oz. simple syrup

½ oz. orange curacao

1 oz. Bacardi light rum

½ oz. Bacardi 151 rum or 1 oz. Bacardi dark or Gold Reserve rum

mint sprig for garnish

pineapple stick for garnish

cherry for garnish

Pour first four ingredients into an old-fashioned or stem glass half-filled with finely cracked ice. Add Bacardi rums and stir gently once or twice. Garnish with mint sprig, pineapple stick, and a cherry. If desired, Mai Tai mix can be substituted for the first four ingredients.

BACARDI MANHATTAN

2–3 oz. Bacardi dark or Gold Reserve rum

1 oz. sweet vermouth

dash Angostura bitters

cherry for garnish

Stir with cracked ice and strain into a cocktail glass or pour over rocks. Garnish with cherry.

BACARDI MARGARITA

1 oz. Bacardi light rum

½ oz. triple sec

1 oz. fresh-squeezed lemon or lime juice

cracked ice

salt to rim glass

Moisten cocktail glass rim with lemon or lime rind. Dip rim in salt. Shake and strain into salt-rimmed glass.

BACARDI MARY

1½ oz. Bacardi light or dark rum

5 oz. tomato juice

squeeze of lemon or lime

dash Worcestershire sauce

pinch salt and pepper

Serve in a large glass over ice cubes. If desired, a prepared mix can be substituted for the last four ingredients.

BACARDI MONKEY WRENCH

2 oz. Bacardi light rum

grapefruit juice to fill

Pour Bacardi light rum into a tall glass over ice. Fill with grapefruit juice. Stir.

BACARDI NAVY GROG

2/3 oz. Bacardi light rum

11/3 oz. Bacardi dark rum

1 oz. fresh lime or lemon juice

1 oz. orange juice

1 oz. pineapple juice

1 oz. passion fruit nectar

½ oz. Falernum syrup

mint sprigs for garnish

Blend with ½ cup finely cracked ice. Pour (unstrained) into a large old-fashioned glass half filled with finely cracked ice. Garnish with mint sprigs and serve with straws.

BACARDI OLD-FASHIONED

1 tsp. sugar

2 tsp. Angostura bitters

splash club soda

Bacardi dark or Gold Reserve rum

sliced fruit for garnish

Dissolve first three ingredients in an old-fashioned glass. Add 2 ice cubes and fill with Bacardi dark or Gold Reserve rum. Garnish with desired fruit slices.

BACARDI ORANGE DAIQUIRI

1½ oz. Bacardi light rum

½ oz. lime or lemon juice

1 oz. orange juice

1 tsp. sugar

Blend with ½ cup crushed ice. Serve in a chilled cocktail glass.

BACARDI PEACH DAIQUIRI

3 oz. Bacardi light rum

2 fresh peach halves, peeled (or 2 canned peach halves)

1 tsp. sugar (omit sugar if using canned peaches)

1 oz. lime or lemon juice

Blend with ½ cup crushed ice. Serve in chilled cocktail glasses. Serves 2. This is the official drink of the National Peach Council.

BACARDI PERFECT MANHATTAN

2–3 oz. Bacardi dark or Gold Reserve rum

½ part dry vermouth

½ part sweet vermouth

dash Angostura bitters

lemon or orange twist for garnish

Stir with cracked ice and strain into a cocktail glass or pour over rocks. Garnish with lemon or orange twist.

BACARDI PIÑA COLADA

1½ oz. Bacardi light or dark rum

1 oz. Coco Lopez real cream of coconut

2 oz. unsweetened pineapple juice

Blend with ½ cup ice or shake and serve over ice.

BACARDI PINEAPPLE
DAIQUIRI

2 oz. Bacardi light rum

½ slice canned pineapple

1 tbsp. lime juice

1 tsp. sugar

Blend with 1/3cup crushed ice. Serve in a chilled cocktail glass.

BACARDI PINK SQUEEZE

1½ oz. Bacardi light rum

pink lemonade to fill

Pour rum into a tall glass over ice and fill with pink lemonade.

BACARDI PLANTER'S PUNCH

3 oz. Bacardi dark or Gold Reserve rum

2 tsp. sugar

2 oz. lemon or lime juice

cherry for garnish

lemon or lime slice for garnish

½ orange, sliced, for garnish

mint sprig for garnish

Dissolve sugar in lemon or lime juice in a shaker. Fill with cracked ice and shake well. Strain into a 10-oz. glass over cracked ice. Garnish with cherry, lemon or lime slice, sliced orange, and a mint sprig. Serve with a straw.

BACARDI QUICK EGGNOG

5 oz. Bacardi dark or light rum

1 pint vanilla or eggnog ice cream

grated nutmeg for garnish

Blend. Sprinkle with nutmeg and serve immediately. Serves 6.

BACARDI RICKEY

2 oz. Bacardi light rum

½ lime or lemon

club soda to fill

Squeeze ½ lime or lemon and drop into a tall glass with ice. Add Bacardi light rum. Fill with club soda. Stir.

BACARDI SCORPION

7 oz. Bacardi light rum

1/3 oz. gin

1/3 oz. brandy

2 oz. orgeat syrup

2 oz. orange juice

4 oz. lemon juice

1 sprig mint

Pour into a pitcher and stir well. Add ice cubes and refrigerate at least an hour before serving in large champagne-type glasses. For a real Polynesian touch, float a gardenia on top. Serves 2.

BACARDI SINGLE EGGNOG

1 oz. Bacardi dark or light rum

1 egg

1 tsp. sugar

8 oz. milk

grated nutmeg for garnish

Shake vigorously with ice and strain into a tall glass. Sprinkle with nutmeg.

BACARDI SOMBRERO COOLER

2 oz. Bacardi light rum

3 oz. pineapple-grapefruit juice

orange, lemon, or lime slice for garnish

Pour over ice. Garnish with orange, lemon, or lime slice.

BACARDI STINGER

2 oz. Bacardi dark rum

1 oz. white crème de menthe

Shake with ice. Serve in a brandy snifter.

BACARDI STRAWBERRY COLADA

1½ oz. Bacardi light or dark rum

1 oz. Coco Lopez real cream of coconut

6 strawberries

Blend with ½ cup ice or shake and serve on ice.

BACARDI STRAWBERRY DAIQUIRI

1½ oz. Bacardi light rum

5 large fresh or frozen whole strawberries

1 tbsp. lime juice

1 tsp. sugar

Blend with ½ cup crushed ice. Serve in a chilled cocktail glass.

BACARDI SUNSET

1¼ oz. Bacardi light rum

orange juice

lime squeeze

orange wheel for garnish

Pour Bacardi light rum into a tall glass over crushed ice. Fill with orange juice and top with a lime squeeze. Garnish with orange wheel.

BACARDI SUPERIOR & GINGER ALE

1 part Bacardi Superior rum

4 parts ginger ale

lime wedge for garnish

Pour over ice in tall glass. Garnish with lime wedge.

BACARDI ZOMBIE

1 oz. Bacardi dark rum

2 oz. Bacardi light rum

1 oz. Bacardi 151 rum (plus ¼ oz. to float, optional)

1 oz. orange juice

1 oz. pineapple juice

juice of 1 lemon or lime

pineapple slice for garnish

cherry for garnish

1 tsp. powdered sugar (optional)

Shake with ice and pour into tall glass. Garnish with pineapple slice and cherry. If desired, float ¼oz. Bacardi 151 and 1 tsp. powdered sugar on top.

BAHAMA MAMA

1½ oz. Whaler's Great White rum

1½ oz. Whaler's Vanille rum

1½ oz. Whaler's Rare Reserve rum

2 oz. pineapple juice

2 oz. orange juice

2 oz. sour mix

dash grenadine (optional)

maraschino cherries for garnish

orange slice for garnish

Shake well with ice. If using grenadine, add to the bottom of the serving glass before pouring. Pour into a chilled hurricane glass. Garnish with maraschino cherries, orange slice, and an umbrella.

BALI HAI

1 oz. Seven Tiki rum

½ oz. ginger liqueur

2 oz. lychee juice

2 oz. pineapple juice

4 mint leaves

mint sprig for garnish

Shake and pour into a highball glass. Garnish with a mint sprig.

BANAN-ALOHA KOOLER

2 oz. Whaler's Big Island banana rum

2 oz. orange juice

2 oz. pineapple juice

strawberry for garnish

Blend or shake with crushed ice. Pour into a cold glass. Garnish with strawberry.

BANANA APPEAL

2 oz. Whaler's Big Island banana rum

2 oz. milk

1 squirt chocolate syrup

1 scoop vanilla ice cream

BANANA BAY BREEZE

2 oz. Malibu Tropical banana rum

1 oz. pineapple juice

1 oz. cranberry juice

orange slice for garnish

Garnish with an orange slice.

Developed by Sapa's, NYC.

BANANA CABANA COSMO

2 oz. Malibu Tropical banana rum

3 oz. tonic water

½ oz. cranberry juice

cherry for garnish

Shake with ice and serve in a tall glass. Garnish with cherry.

Developed by Bamboo 52, NYC.

BANANA COLADA

2 oz. Cruzan banana rum

1½ oz. coconut milk

1½ oz. pineapple juice

Blend with ice until smooth.

BANANA DAIQUIRI

1¼oz. Bacardi light rum

¼ oz. lemon juice or Rose's lime juice

½ tsp. sugar

1 banana

Blend.

BANANA FIESTA

1 oz. Whaler's Big Island banana rum

1 oz. Two Fingers tequila

½ oz. triple sec

3 oz. sweet and sour mix

splash lime juice

Shake with ice and serve in a hurricane glass.

BANANA MAMA

1½ oz. light rum

½ oz. dark rum

1 oz. banana liqueur

1 oz. Coco Lopez real cream of coconut

1 oz. fresh or frozen strawberries

2 oz. pineapple juice

Blend.

BANANA MAN

1 oz. Bacardi light rum

¼ oz. Hiram Walker banana liqueur

½ oz. lemon juice or Rose's lime juice

Blend.

BANANA MILKSHAKE

1 oz. Gosling's gold rum

1 oz. Gosling's Black Seal rum

2 ripe bananas

1 oz. honey

1 cup milk

2 scoops vanilla ice cream

whipped cream for garnish

chocolate syrup for drizzling

Blend with ice and pour into a glass. Garnish with whipped cream. Drizzle chocolate syrup on top.

BANANA PUNCH FRAPPE

1 ½ oz. Bacardi light rum

¾ oz. orange juice

½ oz. banana liqueur

Blend.

BANANA RUM CREAM

1½ oz. Puerto Rican dark rum

½ oz. crème de bananas

1 oz. light cream

Shake well.

BANANA WITH MILK RUM

2 oz. Rhum Barbancourt 3 Stars

1 ripe banana

8½ oz. milk

2 tbsp. powdered sugar

1 egg yolk

Cut the banana into pieces. Beat the egg yolk. Blend all ingredients until a homogenous and consistent mixture is obtained. Pour into a glass and serve.

BARBADOS COCKTAIL

2 oz. Mount Gay rum

½ oz. Cointreau

½ oz. sweet and sour mix

Shake.

BARBADOS PUNCH

2/3 oz. Tommy Bahama Golden Sun rum

1 oz. Tommy Bahama White Sand rum

1/3 oz. premium orange liqueur

1¾ pineapple juice

1¾ orange juice

juice of ½ lime

2 dashes grenadine

orange slice for garnish

maraschino cherry for garnish

Pour all ingredients except Tommy Bahama Golden Sun rum into a shaker over ice. Shake sharply. Strain into a glass over ice. Carefully float Tommy Bahama Golden Sun rum on top. Garnish with slice of orange and maraschino cherry. Serve with a straw.

BARN RAISER

1 oz. light rum

1 oz. Boru vodka

½ oz. grenadine

2 oz. orange juice

2 oz. pineapple juice

¾ oz. Sea Wynde rum

Pour first five ingredients into a glass over ice. Float the Sea Wynde rum.

BEACH BUM'S COOLER

¾ oz. light rum

1¼ oz. Irish cream

¼ oz. banana liqueur

1½ oz. Coco Lopez real cream of coconut

¼ oz. banana

2 scoops vanilla ice cream

maraschino cherry for garnish

Garnish with maraschino cherry.

BEACH PARTY

1¼ oz. Bacardi light or dark rum

1 oz. pineapple juice

1 oz. orange juice

1 oz. Rose's grenadine

Blend.

BEACHCOMBER

1½ oz. Puerto Rican white rum

¾ oz. Rose's lime juice

¼ OZ. triple sec

dash maraschino liqueur

Shake.

BEACHCOMBER'S GOLDDUST

1½ oz. light rum

1 oz. lime juice

½ oz. triple sec

1 oz. Coco Lopez real cream of coconut

½ tsp. sugar

Blend.

BEACHCOMBER'S SPECIAL

1½ oz. Bacardi light rum

½ oz. orange curacao

¾ oz. lemon or lime juice

¼ tsp. sugar (optional)

Blend with crushed ice.

BEE BITE COCKTAIL

1 oz. light rum

juice of 2 limes

2 oz. orange juice

2 tsp. grenadine

Blend with crushed ice.

BEE'S KISS

1 oz. Puerto Rican white rum

¼ oz. Myers's dark rum

¾ oz. cream

2 tbsp. honey

Shake.

BELLA DONNA

1 oz. Gosling's Black Seal rum

1 oz. Disaronno amaretto

2 tbsp. fresh sour mix (combine 1 tbsp. each: sugar, water, lemon juice, lime juice)

Rim martini glass with sugar mix. Shake with ice. Strain into glass and serve.

From the Las Vegas Bellagio Hotel.

THE BERMUDA DREAMSICLE

2 oz. Gosling's Black Seal rum

2 oz. Navan vanilla liqueur

2 oz. orange juice

1 scoop sherbet or orange twist for garnish

Shake vigorously with ice and strain into a martini glass. Garnish with a small scoop of sherbet or an orange twist.

BERMUDA TRIANGLE

1½ oz. Admiral Nelson's premium vanilla rum

2 oz. cranberry juice

2 oz. orange juice

orange slice for garnish

Stir gently over ice and garnish with a fresh orange slice.

THE BERMUDIAN

2 oz. Gosling's Gold Bermuda rum

2 oz. pineapple juice

¼ oz. Grand Marnier

2 fresh mint leaves, torn

lime twist for garnish

Shake vigorously and strain into a martini glass. Garnish with twist of lime.

BERRIES 'N' CREAM

½ oz. Captain Morgan Original spiced rum

¾ oz. wild berry schnapps

3 oz. strawberry cocktail mix

2 tbsp. raspberries or strawberries in syrup

2 oz. heavy cream

16 oz. scoop of crushed ice

BERRY MERRY CHRISTMAS

1 oz. RedRum

½ oz. blackberry brandy

5 oz. hot water

½ oz. lemon juice

¼ oz. grenadine

1 cinnamon stick

Combine first five ingredients in a mug and stir with the cinnamon stick.

BETWEEN THE SHEETS

½ oz. Pyrat XO Reserve rum

¼ oz. Citronge

½ oz. Cognac VSOP-Style

1 oz. fresh sweet and sour mix

lemon twist for garnish

sugar to rim glass

Shake and serve straight up in a glass with a sugar-coated rim. Garnish with a lemon twist.

BIG BAMBOO LOVE SONG

2 oz. Whaler's Rare Reserve rum

1 oz. Whalers's Great White rum

½ oz. triple sec

1 oz. pineapple juice

1 oz. orange juice

1 oz. lime juice

¾ oz. fruit syrup

Shake well with ice and pour into a Collins glass.

THE BIGWOOD GIRLS

¾ oz. Puerto Rican light rum

½ oz. brandy

½ oz. Cointreau or triple sec

½ oz. lemon juice

Shake.

BIKINI DAIQUIRI

¾ oz. Cruzan pineapple rum

¾ oz. Cruzan banana rum

2 oz. Coco Lopez real cream of coconut

1 oz. lime juice

Blend with crushed ice.

BLACK BEAUTY

1½ oz. Gosling's Black Seal rum

2–3 ripe blackberries

juice of ½ lime

1 sugar cube

2 dashes Peychaud bitters

2–3 oz. soda water

Muddle the blackberries, sugar cube, bitters, and lime juice. Add Gosling's Black Seal rum and shake with ice. Strain into a glass over fresh ice and top with soda water.

Created by the Old Sealbach Bar.

BLACK DEVIL

1½ oz. Puerto Rican light rum

½ oz. dry vermouth

1 pitted black olive

Stir well.

BLACK ELEPHANT

1 oz. Gosling's Black Seal rum

1 oz. Amarula cream liqueur

Pour over ice and stir.

BLACK JACK

Equal parts:

Gosling's Black Seal rum

Jack Daniels, chilled

BLACK MARIA

1 oz. Myers's dark rum

¾ oz. Tia Maria

1 tsp. sugar

1 cup cold coffee

lemon peel

Stir.

BLACK SEAL RUM RUNNER

1¼oz. Gosling's Black Seal rum

¾ oz. blackberry liqueur

1 oz. banana liqueur

¾ oz. grenadine

½ oz. lime juice

Blend with crushed ice.

BLIGHTER BOB

1 oz. Puerto Rican light rum

½ oz. Puerto Rican dark rum

½ oz. créme de cassis

1 oz. orange juice

2 dashes orange bitters

2 oz. ginger ale

lemon twist

Stir.

BLING BLING

1 oz. RedRum

1 oz. Hypnotiq

2 oz. pineapple juice

2 oz. 7UP

Shake with ice and strain into a shot glass.

BLUE HAWAIIAN

1 oz. Tommy Bahama White Sand rum

1 oz. blue curacao

2 oz. pineapple juice

1 oz. coconut cream

pineapple slice for garnish

maraschino cherry for garnish

Blend with a scoop of crushed ice until smooth. Strain into a glass. Garnish with a slice of fresh pineapple and a maraschino cherry.

BLUE HEAVEN

1 oz. light rum

1 oz. Hiram Walker blue curacao

1 oz. pineapple juice

1 tsp. Coco Lopez real cream of coconut

Blend with crushed ice.

BLUE LAGOON

1½ oz. Appleton Estate V/X Jamaica rum

4 oz. cranberry juice

lemon wedge for garnish

Stir with crushed ice. Serve in a cocktail glass and garnish with a wedge of lemon.

BLUE LIZARD

2 oz. Cruzan citrus rum

¾ oz. blue curacao

¼ oz. sweet and sour mix

¼ oz. Sprite or 7UP

Pour the first two ingredients into a glass over ice. Add sweet and sour and Sprite or 7UP. Stir and serve.

BLUE MARLIN

1 shot blue curaçao

1 shot Whaler's Great White rum

4 oz. lemon-lime mix

lime slice for garnish

Shake well over ice and strain into a chilled rocks glass. Garnish with lime slice.

BLUE PASSION

¾ oz. Captain Morgan Original spiced rum

½ oz. blue curacao

4 oz. sweet and sour mix

pineapple slice for garnish

Shake well with an 8-oz. scoop of crushed ice and serve in a Collins glass. Garnish with a pineapple slice.

BLUE SKY

¾ oz. Bacardi light rum

1½ oz. Canadian Mist

¾ oz. blue curacao

8 oz. pineapple juice

orange slice for garnish

maraschino cherry for garnish

Blend with crushed ice. Garnish with an orange slice and a maraschino cherry.

BLUE SUNSET

2 oz. Whaler's Pineapple Paradise rum

2 oz. pineapple juice

½ oz. blue curacao

Shake well and serve in a martini glass.

BLUE WATCH

¾ oz. Captain Morgan Original spiced rum

½ oz. blue curacao

4 oz. ginger ale

Pour over rocks in old-fashioned glass. Stir lightly.

BOB'S YOUR UNCLE

2 oz. Wray & Nephew rum

½ oz. Frangelico

½ oz. Cuarenta Tres liquor

¼ oz. Funkin liquid chocolate

¼ oz. white Mozart chocolate liquor

white chocolate for garnish

Lace chilled cocktail glass with white Mozart chocolate liquor. Shake all other ingredients and pour into the cocktail glass with Mozart chocolate liquor. Garnish with white chocolate.

THE BODEGA

2 oz. 10 Cane rum

2 oz. Coco Lopez real cream of coconut

2 oz. mango nectar

2 oz. guava nectar

Combine all ingredients in a mixing glass. Add ice and shake vigorously. Strain into a chilled classic daiquiri glass. May also be served unstrained in a rocks glass.

Created by: Robert Ryan, New York City mixologist.

BOGART'S AFRICAN QUEEN

3 oz. Starr African rum

3 oz. Alizé passion fruit

Shake well over ice and strain into a martini glass.

BOLERO

1½ oz. Rhum Barbancourt

½ oz. Calvados

2 tsp. sweet vermouth

dash bitters

Stir. Serve straight up or on the rocks.

BONBINI

1 oz. Bacardi light or dark rum

¼ oz. Hiram Walker orange curaçao

2 dashes Angostura bitters

Stir.

BONE SHAKER

2 oz. VooDoo spiced rum

½ oz. triple sec

½ oz. lime juice

3 oz. pineapple juice

lime wedge for garnish

Blend with crushed ice. Garnish with lime wedge.

BONGO DRUM

1 oz. Bacardi light rum

¼ oz. Hiram Walker blackberry-flavored brandy

pineapple juice to fill

Pour rum into a tall glass half filled with ice. Fill with pineapple juice. Float brandy on top.

BONSAI COLADA

3 oz. Whaler's Pineapple Paradise rum

1 oz. Burnett's orange vodka

1 oz. coconut cream

pineapple slice for garnish

Shake with ice and strain or pour into a hurricane glass. Garnish with pineapple slice.

BORINQUEN

1½ oz. light rum

1 tbsp. passion fruit syrup

1 oz. lime juice

1 oz. orange juice

1 tsp. 151-proof rum

Blend at low speed with ½ cup crushed ice. Pour into an old-fashioned glass.

BOSSA NOVA

2 oz. dark rum

1½ oz. Liquore Galliano

1 oz. apricot brandy

3 oz. passion fruit juice

BOSTON BREEZE

1¼ oz. rum

1 oz. Coco Lopez real cream of coconut

3 oz. cranberry juice cocktail

Blend with crushed ice.

BOSTON COOLER

2 oz. light rum

juice of ½ lemon

1 tsp. powdered sugar

2 oz. club soda

club soda or ginger ale to fill

orange spiral or lemon peel for garnish

Pour first three ingredients into a Collins glass and stir. Fill with cracked ice and add rum. Fill with club soda or ginger ale and stir again. Garnish with a spiral of orange or lemon peel and dangle end over rim of glass.

BOSTON SIDECAR

¾ oz. light rum

¾ oz. brandy

¾ oz. triple sec

juice of ½ lime

Shake with ice and strain into a cocktail glass.

BRAND NEW TATTOO

2 oz. Sailor Jerry Navy spiced rum

7UP to fill

splash orange juice

Pour Sailor Jerry Navy spiced rum into a glass and fill with 7UP. Mix. Add a splash of orange juice.

BRIDGETOWN

2 oz. Cockspur Fine rum

splash cherry juice

dash sweet vermouth

cherry for garnish

Shake with ice. Serve in a cocktail glass. Garnish with cherry.

BRINLEY COFFEE ON THE ROCKS

3 oz. Brinley gold coffee rum

crushed ice

fresh coffee bean for garnish

Garnish with coffee bean.

BRINLEY CREAMSICLE

2 oz. Brinley vanilla rum

2 oz. orange juice

1 oz. milk

Shake well and pour into a glass over ice.

BRINLEY LIME FIZZ

3 parts Brinley Gold lime rum

4 parts club soda or lemon-lime soda

lime wedge for garnish

Pour into a tall glass over ice. Garnish with lime wedge.

BRINLEY "SPIKED" HOT COCOA

3 oz. Brinley Gold vanilla rum

4 oz. hot hot chocolate

1 marshmallow (or 6 small marshmallows)

chocolate shavings for garnish

Serve piping hot in a big mug. Top off with marshmallow and dark chocolate shavings.

BROWN DERBY

1¼oz. Puerto Rican dark rum

½ oz. lime juice

1/6 oz. maple syrup

Shake.

BUBBLES & MANGO

1 oz. mango puree

2 oz. Flor de Cana 7-year-old rum

¾ oz. fresh-squeezed lime juice

½ oz. simple syrup

1½ oz. Prosecco

Shake first four ingredients and strain into a 6-oz. martini glass. Top with Prosecco.

BUCK-A-ROO

1¼ oz. Bacardi light or dark rum

root beer to fill

Pour rum into a highball glass over ice. Fill with root beer.

BUCK JONES

1½ oz. light rum

1 oz. sweet sherry

juice of ½ lime

ginger ale to fill

Pour first three ingredients into a highball glass over ice cubes and stir. Fill with ginger ale.

BULLDOG COCKTAIL

1½ oz. Bacardi light or dark rum

¾ oz. lime juice

½ oz. cherry-flavored brandy

maraschino cherry for garnish

Garnish with maraschino cherry.

BURGUNDY BISHOP

1 oz. light rum

juice of ¼ lemon

1 tsp. powdered sugar

red wine to fill

fresh fruit for garnish

Shake with ice and strain into a highball glass over ice cubes. Fill with red wine and stir. Decorate with fruits.

BUSHRANGER

1 oz. Puerto Rican white rum

1 oz. Dubonnet

2 dashes Angostura bitters

Stir.

BUSHWHACKER

½ oz. rum

2 oz. Coco Lopez real cream of coconut

1 oz. coffee-flavored liqueur

½ oz. dark crème de cacao

2 oz. half and half

Blend with 1 cup ice until smooth.

BWI SWIZZLE

2 oz. Pyrat XO Reserve rum

½ oz. Marie Brizard Apry liqueur

1 oz. Rock Candy syrup or simple syrup

juice of 1 lime

2 dashes Angtostura bitters

Pour into a 14-oz. goblet ¾full with crushed ice. Put a swizzle between the palms of your hands and swizzle, adding crushed ice until the drink is frothing and the outside of the glass frosts.

THE CAESAR'S KISS

½ oz. Bacardi vanilla rum

1 oz. Tequila Rose

½ oz. Baileys Irish cream

½ oz. Chambord

strawberry whipped cream for garnish

Shake. Serve in a rocks glass. Garnish with strawberry whipped cream.

CAFE RUMBA

1 oz. Kahlua

1 oz. Whaler's Vanille rum

hot coffee to fill

whipped cream to top

Pour first two ingredients into a mug. Fill with coffee. Top with whipped cream and enjoy.

CAIPIRISSIMA

2 oz. Pyrat Superior Blanco rum

1 small lime, cut into quarters

1 heaping tsp. brown sugar

In a 16-oz. mixing glass muddle the lime and brown sugar together until juice has been extracted and the sugar dissolved. Fill with cracked (not crushed) ice, then add Pyrat Superior Blanco rum. Shake until well blended and pour into a double old-fashioned glass. Add more ice if needed.

CALIFORNIA FIZZ

1½ oz. Bacardi light or dark rum

4 oz. orange juice

club soda to top

Pour first two ingredients into a tall glass. Top with club soda.

CALM BEFORE THE STORM

2½ oz. Tommy Bahama Golden Sun rum

juice of ½ lime

ginger beer to top

lime wheel for garnish

Pour first two ingredients into a bucket glass over ice. Top with ginger beer. Garnish with lime wheel.

CALM VOYAGE

1 oz. Bacardi light rum

¼ oz. Hiram Walker apple-flavored brandy

1 oz. orange juice

dash bitters

Shake with ice and serve on the rocks.

CALYPSO COOL-AID

1¼ oz. Rhum Barbancourt

1 oz. pineapple juice

½ oz. lemon or lime juice

¼ tsp. sugar

club soda to top

Blend first four ingredients. Top with club soda. Garnish with pineapple spear and lime wheel.

CALYPSO COOLER

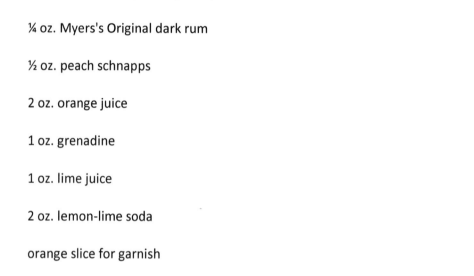

½ oz. Captain Morgan Original spiced rum

¼ oz. Myers's Original dark rum

½ oz. peach schnapps

2 oz. orange juice

1 oz. grenadine

1 oz. lime juice

2 oz. lemon-lime soda

orange slice for garnish

Shake first six ingredients well and pour into a Collins or specialty glass over ice. Top with lemon-lime soda. Garnish with an orange slice.

CANA BRAVA

2 oz. Flor de Cana Gold 4-year-old rum

3 oz. Bloody Mary mix

½ oz. jalapeno juice

½ oz. lime juice

Stir over ice.

CANA DORADA MARTINI

½ oz. sweetened lime juice

1½ oz. Flor de Cana gold 7-year-old rum

½ oz. triple sec

1 oz. orange juice

Shake and serve in a martini glass.

CANA-SUTRA

2 oz. Flor de Cana extra-dry 4-year-old rum

1 oz. cranberry juice

1 oz. pineapple juice

1 oz. peach schnapps

1 oz. grenadine

Shake and serve on the rocks.

THE CANARY

1½ oz. 10 Cane rum

1½ oz. anisette

2½ oz. fresh-squeezed pineapple juice

crème de cacao to rim glass

brown sugar to rim glass

1 star anise for garnish

Rim a martini glass with crème de cacao and brown sugar. Pour 10 Cane, anisette, and pineapple juice into a shaker with ice. Shake vigorously and strain into the martini glass. Garnish with a floating star anise. Recline in an armchair.

Created by the Elbow Beach Resort bartender team, Bermuda.

CANITAS

2 oz. 10 Cane rum

1 shot espresso

sugar to taste (optional)

1 tsp. fresh whipped cream (optional)

In a small shot or juice glass add 10 Cane and espresso. Add sugar, if using. Garnish with fresh whipped cream, if desired.

CANNONBALL

1–2 oz. Gosling's Black Seal rum

½ oz. Rose's lime cordial

Equal parts (to top):

   cranberry juice

   pineapple juice

   orange juice

orange wheel for garnish

cherry for garnish

Pour the first two ingredients into a glass. Top with equal parts cranberry, pineapple, and orange juice. Garnish with orange wheel and cherry.

CAPTAIN MORGAN DAIQUIRI

1 oz. Captain Morgan Original spiced rum

¼ oz. cherry liqueur

1 oz. sweet and sour mix

lime wheel for garnish

Shake vigorously over crushed ice and strain into a stemmed cocktail glass. Garnish with lime wheel.

CAPTAIN MORGAN SOUR

1 ¼ oz. Captain Morgan Original spiced rum

1 oz. fresh-squeezed lemon juice

1 tsp. sugar

Shake and serve on the rocks.

CAPTAIN'S COLADA

1¼ oz. Captain Morgan Original spiced rum

5 oz. piña colada mix

pineapple stick for garnish

maraschino cherry for garnish

Blend with crushed ice until smooth. Pour into specialty glass. Garnish with pineapple stick and a maraschino cherry.

CAPTAIN'S CRUISER

1¼ oz. Captain Morgan Parrot Bay rum

3 oz. orange juice

2 oz. pineapple juice

Mix in a shaker. Pour into a tall glass over ice.

CAPTAIN'S PEARL

1 oz. Captain Morgan Original spiced rum

¼ oz. amaretto

1½ oz. half and half

½ ripe banana

Blend with a scoop of crushed ice.

CAPTAIN'S TROPICAL SPICED TEA

1¼ oz. Captain Morgan Original spiced rum

3 oz. iced tea

½ tsp. lemon juice

2 oz. ginger ale

lemon wheel for garnish

Stir in a highball glass over ice. Garnish with a lemon wheel.

CARIBBEAN COCOA

1½ oz. Coruba Jamaica rum

hot cocoa to fill

whipped cream for garnish

chocolate curls for garnish

Pour Coruba rum into a mug. Fill with hot cocoa. Garnish with whipped cream and top with chocolate curls.

CARIBBEAN COOLER

1 oz. Captain Morgan Original spiced rum

¼ oz. white créme de cacao

3 oz. orange juice

1½ oz. club soda

Pour rum, créme de cacao, and orange juice over ice in a glass. Stir. Add soda and stir gently.

CARIBBEAN CRUSH

3 oz. coconut milk

1/3 ripe banana

½ oz. Baileys Irish cream

1½ oz. Pyrat XO Reserve rum

1 scoop of ice

whipped cream for garnish

shredded coconut for garnish

Blend for 15–20 seconds. Garnish with whipped cream and shredded coconut.

CARIBBEAN DATE

1½ oz. Pyrat XO Reserve rum

1 oz. tangerine puree

1 oz. Thai coconut milk

cinnamon and demerara sugar to rim glass

mint sprig for garnish

Shake with ice and strain into a chilled cocktail glass rimmed with cinnamon-demerara sugar. Garnish with a fresh mint sprig.

CARIBBEAN JOY

1½ oz. Bacardi light rum

1 oz. pineapple juice

¾ oz. lemon juice

Shake and serve on the rocks.

CARIBBEAN PASSION

½ oz. Mount Gay rum

¾ oz. Passoã

1 oz. pineapple juice

splash orange juice

Shake. Serve in a tall glass over ice.

CARIBBEAN QUEEN

1¼ oz. Bacardi Limón rum

½ oz. Cointreau

2 oz. orange juice

3 oz. Coco Lopez real cream of coconut

Blend with ice. Serve in a martini glass.

CARIBBEAN ROMANCE

3 oz. Bacardi light rum

1½ oz. sugar syrup

2 pieces papaya

2 pieces banana

1 oz. lime juice

1 oz. Coco Lopez real cream of coconut

orange slice for garnish

pineapple slice for garnish

cherry for garnish

Blend. Garnish with orange slice, pineapple slice, and cherry.

CARIBBEAN SEA

1½ oz. Appleton Estate V/X Jamaica rum

¾ oz. blue curacao

3 oz. pineapple juice

1½ oz. coconut cream

Mix in a Collins glass over ice.

CARIBBEAN SHOOTER

¾ oz. Captain Morgan Original spiced rum

½ oz. brandy

1 oz. cranberry juice

Shake with ice and strain into a glass.

CARIBBEAN SUNSET

¾ oz. Whaler's Great white rum

¾ oz. Burnett's gin

¾ oz. blue curaçao

¾ oz. banana liqueur

1 oz. lemon juice

1 oz. lime juice

dash grenadine

lime slice for garnish

Shake first six ingredients over ice and pour into a cocktail glass. Add grenadine and garnish with lime slice.

CARIBE COCKTAIL

1¼ oz. Captain Morgan Original spiced rum

1 oz. pineapple juice

½ oz. lemon juice

lime wedge for garnish

Shake with ice cubes and strain into a stemmed cocktail glass. Garnish with lime wedge.

CARNIVAL COOLER

2 oz. Fernandes "19" white rum

¾ oz. lime juice

2 dashes Angostura bitters

club soda to fill

Pour first three ingredients into a Collins glass over ice and stir. Fill with club soda.

CASABLANCA

2 oz. Captain Morgan Original spiced rum

½ oz. créme de noya

¼ oz. apricot liqueur

4 oz. orange juice

½ oz. simple syrup

Serve in a glass with a 6-oz. scoop of crushed ice.

CHAMBORD COLADA

1½ oz. Bacardi rum

1½ oz. Chambord

2 oz. pineapple juice

½ oz. Coco Lopez real cream of coconut

Blend with ice. Serve in a tall glass.

CHAMPAGNE TIKI

1 oz. Pyrat XO Reserve rum

1 oz. Cruzan banana rum

1 oz. fresh strawberry coulis

juice of ½ lime

champagne to top

grated nutmeg for garnish

mint sprig for garnish

Shake first four ingredients and strain into a 7½ -oz. stem glass. Top with champagne. Garnish with a sprinkle of nutmeg and fresh mint sprig.

CHAYOTE SPECIAL

1½ oz. Bacardi light rum

3 drops blue curacao

1½ oz. sour apple

green apple slice for garnish

Shake with cracked ice until cold. Serve in a chilled martini glass and garnish with a slice of green apple.

From the Chayote Restaurant.

CHERRIED CREAM RUM

1½ oz. Rhum Barbancourt

½ oz. cherry brandy

½ oz. light cream

Shake.

COCOA BEACH

1½ Prichards's Crystal rum

4 oz. orange juice

2 oz. pineapple juice

1 oz. piña colada mix

Blend with ¾ cup ice until slushy.

COCOBANA

1 part Bacardi light rum

1 banana

1 part coconut milk

Blend with crushed ice.

Susan McGowan, Oddfellows Restaurant.

COCOMOTION

1½ oz. Puerto Rican dark rum

4 oz. Coco Lopez real cream of coconut

2 oz. lime juice

Blend with 1 ½ cups ice.

COCONUT BANANA COLADA

2 oz. Cruzan coconut rum

¾ oz. Cruzan banana rum

2 oz. Coco Lopez real cream of coconut

3 oz. pineapple juice

Blend with crushed ice.

COCONUT BROWNIE

1¼ oz. Captain Morgan Original spiced rum

¼ oz. hot chocolate

1 tsp. whipped cream

Pour first two ingredients into a mug and top with whipped cream.

COCONUT CLOUD MARTINI

1 oz. Tommy Bahama White Sand rum

½ oz. vanilla vodka

½ oz. coconut rum

½ oz. Coco Lopez real cream of coconut

toasted coconut for garnish

Shake with ice. Garnish with toasted coconut.

Milton Keynes UK
Ingram Content Group UK Ltd.
UKHW010750110923
428455UK00014B/756